Bird Calls

Bird Calls

POEMS BY

Maria Mello

FOUR SQUARE PRESS
BOSTON, MASSACHUSETTS

Published by Four Square Press
85 Devonshire Street, 11th Floor
Boston, MA 02109
www.foursquarepress.com

ISBN 978-0-9851689-2-6
Library of Congress Control Number: 2012948414

Contents

CHIMNEY SWIFTS:

THE SWARM:

White-Winged Gulls

WHITE-WINGED GULLS

To see them
requires a fine madness
such as possessed only by those
who are filled
    with the restlessness of winter
    and the void.
We stand on the rocky jetty
    where the frozen winds scream
    over an icy slate sea
    with violent blasts and power.
We search through the gull congregations
    while our eyes fill with tears
    and our noses grow numb
    and our bodies protest with pain
    against the punishment of cold.
But every winter one, two, or three return
    the ivory and the glaucous gulls
    not many
    but enough to fill the promise.
White as the winter winds they soar
    to mix with the common gulls
    and repeatedly lure us back
    to the lonely, icy shore.

THE DEVIL TREE

It stood beside a pond,
a wild place where beavers worked
and otters slid playfully down the banks.
A holy place.
I saw it every springtime,
when the ground oozed mud
and ice still hid in shady crevices.
And I greeted it with anger...
    the devil tree.

It wasn't meant
(as anyone could see)
to be a tree.
Tree bark is gray and brown,
dark or white,
or muted earthy colors
caught in sun-crossed shadows,
well scarred by life
and flaunting the bruises of existence.
But this tree's bark was green,
smooth with slashed stripes of lighter green
and leaves like large geese feet,
not lacy, not fluttering...just odd.

Summers
were never lonely times
just good.
Sitting under its sheltering shade

I watched fish jumping in the water,
saw the hummingbird come to her nest,
felt a dragonfly land on my bare arm,
heard the slap of a beaver's tail.
And the devil tree and I
made cautious friends.
I went to it late last springtime.
Snow staying long on the land
and a cold sorrow smothering my heart
kept me long away
from the still, brown pond.

When I went at last
blood root glowed
at the feet of dark trees
and warblers trilled with joy
as butterflies splashed color in the sun.

Our greeting was a cautious, hushed hello.
I reached to stroke the smooth green bark
and looking up
saw empty sky
peering through bare branches.

There were no leaves.

My point of constancy
in the ever-changing forest,
the devil tree,
was dead.
Too late...

it is always too late
we learn what to hold close.
Too late...
it is always too late.
I loved
the devil tree.

Owl Woods

Darkness drips
    from the tall, still pines
and crusted snow lies in patches.
The air blows warm, then cold
touched by the sun
yet still chilled from winter winds
    and ice.

No birds sing.
    But a deer keeps me in his sight
    while he strips bark from a young tree.
I walk softly on the slippery needles
looking at trees, feeling the stillness,
feeling the peace.

One tree stands out.
White splashes drip down its trunk
and looking up, my eyes meet those
of the great horned owl in her nest.

I move back to see her better.
Her nest is a ragged mass of leaves and twigs
stolen from a lesser bird or squirrel
earlier in the season.
She watches me coldly, still and hushed.
If I press too closely and try to climb the tree
    (a most unlikely scene)
she will attack, her wings silent,

her voice still.
A flurry of feathers pops up beside her
then sinks back down.
At least one young is there with her.

The owl and I watch each other with respect.
Wrapped in the quiet, cool freshness
of the February woods
we keep vigil
safe
in the gentle pines.

WATER

A circle of silver catches my eyes
in the nighttime garden.
It is only the moon caught
in the fresh-filled bird bath.

Michael Has Gone Away

He knows me, he might know you,
 if he ever knew you.
His smile remains sweet,
 sweet, and patient with he world.

He remembers...
flying over Germany somewhere, sometime...
 was it yesterday?
His plane caught in searchlights...
a cacophony of explosions and gunfire,
and the parachute, a white dome,
easing him down through the stars.

He knows...
 the house where he raised his children
with her
the only woman he ever loved.

He is a simple, kind old man.
 He is a young boy, scared and alone,
who floats among friendly stars
and looks at the world with innocent eyes.

He smiles his sweet smile...
until his best friend takes him out,
then won't bring him back home,
but brings him back to an apartment
he has never seen before,

though his family pictures are scattered about
and his furniture has been placed there.
Then the smile fades, and he gets angry...
he wants to go home.

Michael is eighteen...
and the parachute blooms open over his head
promising
    a few more hours of life.

But at night
he slips out a side door
    unseen...
and walks the streets
    outside Berlin, inside Peabody,
trying to find his home.
Alone,
    alone in the world.

Then a cruiser stops beside him.
The police will help him...
    the Gestapo will take him.
He gives his name, rank,
and smiles a stream of numbers.
His friends, the stars, are silent.

In Time

In time
 I will grow used to things
I won't reach for him
in the darkest night
knowing
 he will not be there
I'll understand
 so they say.

And where
 we used to sail at dawn
I won't hear his laugh
when I foul the lines
and salt
 won't flavor every kiss
I will accept
 what they say.

In time
 the lilacs in the spring
won't tear at my heart
with their clouds of scent
Springtime
 will come without his smile
I'll heal and grow
 so they say.

In time
    I'll learn to laugh again
in a minor key
It will still be me
crippled
    I'll learn to fly again
They won't say it
    but I know.

And as Time
runs away with me
things will fill my days
in such different ways
than they sweetly
used to be...
I'll still love him...
    this I know.

Veery

VEERY

Once
on a lonely path beside the river Slade
waiting
for evening to fall
and my lover to come,
I heard a veery sing, close by.

And haunting through the glowing woods,
the loneliness was hushed and colored
in elusive rainbows
and dissipated
by the gentle, ghostly song.

Loves are lost or die.
Time erases passion
and what was once eternal
becomes a hazy memory,
a shadow on the soul.
The promise of unending love
is broken...
vanishes...
nothing.

She Smelled of Ivory Soap

When I was a child
   (which is an unsettling statement
    as I feel I'm sometimes still there)
I didn't know about social classes for a long time.
I lived in a blue-collar neighborhood
and went to public school.
When children brought their lunches to school,
some had peanut butter and jelly,
or thin ham and cheese,
chicken salad or tuna salad
on bread with the crusts trimmed off.
My lunch was often a surprise.
There'd be tortas with onions and parsley,
sometimes apple jelly,
baked beans on buttered bread.
And *once* flounder, with mayonnaise...
   Oh God!
Crusts cut off? Never.
We did not buy bread to throw half of it out.
Suppers were often soups...
Not chicken or vegetable or tomato.
Kale, turnip greens
   And fumsch
(which I still grow and still don't know for sure what it is).
Soups with onions, rice, the greens
   sometimes white beans
and always we mixed in hunks of hard bread.
Garlic was our staff of life

on hamburg,
and pork chops,
and fish,
anywhere it could go.
Never on steak or roast beef.
    (I was twenty when I had my first steak
     tough as nails and no garlic taste.)

I dressed in my cousin's hand-me-downs
thrilled to have those "new" clothes.

My long, dark hair was neatly braided.
I was always clean
    or started the day that way,
a boring child perhaps, but happy in my world.
I thought everyone lived in it.

And I had friends...
    Grace, Nancy, Louise, Alicia, Theresa.
Sometimes on Saturdays we'd go uptown,
    go to the movies (double feature),
or drift through Daniel Lowes
    admiring and choosing dishes and silverware,
    crystals and figurines...
    to furnish homes far in the distance,
    homes with husbands we'd never met.

Later we'd stop at Martha's Sweets
    for one of their exotic-sounding candies.

We were all very, very rich then

and didn't know it.
Shop owners didn't cringe when we entered.
We were just kids
    not buyers usually (not in Daniel Lowes anyhow),
    but we weren't rowdy or destructive or thieves.
Most of us had to go to confession later in the day,
except Nancy, who wasn't Catholic.

I don't know why Nancy and I broke our friendship.
By seventh grade it was over.
It must have been a petty misunderstanding
that we were too unskilled to settle.
But just before the friendship ended
I remember walking to her house
to pick her up so we could walk together
to meet Alicia and Grace.
She came down the stairs,
    all freshly cleaned,
her face scrubbed,
her short hair brushed until it glowed.
But mostly I remember the smell...
Ivory Soap.
Not Lava soap,
certainly not onions or garlic.

I crossed a line that day.
That's what a lady should smell like...
    Ivory Soap,
and I was not that lady.

Alicia, our most talented, died young,

her talent buried in the grave.
The rest of us lost touch.
Time erased the past.
I shopped in Daniel Lowes until it closed.
I grew up.

But sometimes when the mood hits
I buy Ivory Soap,
    scrub hard, soak in the sudsy water,
    put on a white cotton nightgown,
    go to bed with a book, but don't read.
Instead I lie there in the soft darkness
    feeling clean,
    and pure,
    and good.
And for a short while
    before it wears off
I, too, smell of Ivory Soap.

Unanswered Questions

I never asked my uncle
what he'd done in the war
(the "war to end all wars")
or where he'd been,
how long he'd stayed,
what he had seen and felt.
But he knew where the mayflowers grew
and never frightened the little girl
who followed him religiously
down winding paths, bushwhacking
when the trails ran out,
a shy child, easily frightened,
but never with him.

I never heard him speak
to the other adults about his time away.
He spoke instead of crops
and the deer in the early morning fields,
of the new calf, jet black and frisky,
and how his turkeys were growing.
Of how he'd signed a ninety-nine year lease
with the power company
to cut a wide swath through his land.
And soon there'd be electricity
to replace the kerosene lanterns
on long winter nights.
But he never mentioned the foreign lands
of that time away,

as if it never were, never had been.

He never warned me against
going anywhere on his land alone, except...
he told me about Dennis,
his fierce German shepherd.
"Don't tease him; he's dangerous."
But when the grownups went inside
I'd lie on the grass,
and Dennis would lie beside me,
two wild, peaceful souls.

Until I got up to cross the road
and walk alone into the woods until the path gave out.
Then Dennis leapt up to join me,
running ahead, gone...then rushing back.

Walking down the road together,
my uncle showed me where
a blacksmith once had his shop.
And he'd tell me of his dream
of building a brand new house
at the far edge of the field,
placing it to get the early morning sun.
But he never built it.
And I learned dreams were like water,
necessary, but you couldn't hold them in your hands.

I wonder, now, as I remember walking those trails
if we were united by innocence....
the child who didn't know about the world,

and the man who'd erased all his yesterdays.

I am so glad
I never asked those questions.

Eating Kale Soup
in the Sunshine

The March wind blows true,
   blows cold,
but around the corner of the yard,
where the witch hazel blazes
   in a refined splash of color,
the house protects,
   and the weathered table waits.
I carry the stoneware mug with care.
Setting it down I caress the warm cup,
smell deeply the rising steam,
   and drift...
       drift...
         drift away.

I am a little girl again
playing in the yard on a snow day,
then running inside with rosy cheeks
to the kitchen, where the big black stove presides,
and the smell of kale soup
   fills the room.
We sit at the table by the big window,
Mama, Daddy, and me,
   not knowing how poor we are
with our big bowls of kale soup
and plates of thick homemade bread.

All gone...long gone,
   the people, the time, the place.

Yet somehow, I think if I turn around quickly
    and reach out,
I can touch those days.

I look down at the mug before me
dark green leaves,
    pale green broth,
    slivers of onions,
    white beans and garbanzo beans.
The words trip up my tongue,
the old Portuguese words come easier.

Once I ate with a family,
now I eat alone.
But as I eat slowly
    (to make it last)
the woman in me fades
and the child comes back
sitting in the March sunshine...
wide-eyed watching the squirrels,
smiling at the chickadees
    squabbling at the feeder,
hearing the sad call of the mourning dove
    with joy,
seeing the snowdrops blooming
    under the lilac bushes.

Nothing lasts...the cup is empty.
The soup brought me back to yesterdays
whose sorrows drift off like the steam
and whose nourishing joys
    feed my body and my soul.

24

First Butterfly

Endless rain has yielded at last
to sun
and flowers
which came up in spite of
spring snow
whipping winds
and saturated earth.
But they came.
From swollen buds they thrust out
into vibrant colors of aching beauty.

And on this Holy Thursday
the first butterfly appears.
A male cabbage butterfly
he flutters
around the perimeter of the yard
respecting the boundaries of driveway and fences
(or ignoring them
as ugly adjuncts of a promised land).

Stopping now and then he rests
on an upright naked branch
then flies on again in jagged spurts
to see if this place in the world will do.
There's water, food, sun and shelter.
He'll show the female all the special nooks.

At last he comes to the table

where I sit, my book unread, my tea forgotten.
I freeze
as he circles, in curiosity?
then pauses on the table across from me.

Just for one second he and I
share a moment of eternity
which is really all we ever get,
moments, like precious jewels
threaded on the string of life.

Woodcock

Woodcock

Though spring is just a whisper on the land
and the earth still slips with mud
and the shadow of winter
yet chills the evening air,
the woodcock begins his flights
    of life
        and love.

His dull "pent" sound is insect-like,
nonmusical at best.
His body
    squat and chunky,
    in variations of brown,
displays no elegance,
    no style,
        no beauty.
He is a basic woodland bird.

But suddenly
a whirring sound cuts the evening air
as up and up and up
in dizzying circles he climbs
making mad, grand loops
against the moon-drenched sky
until he nearly touches it.

Only to dissolve
    down
        down
          down
to start the circle rapture
of love
all over again.

Turk's Cap

As a child I walked
these trails across
the dirt road, through the fields
where daisies laughed,
to the bridge of rough logs
laid tightly side by side,
a little trimmed, but mostly
raw tree trunks.

Then through the pines
which guarded both
sides of the two-rutted
trail that was always
ready to regrow
and turn back to wilderness.

Then the forest opened up
to a large sandy clearing.
The Sand Pit I called it,
about a foot deeper
than the surrounding land,
a good house lot size,
but why or how it came to be,
I never knew or ever asked.

One day, one day only,
I saw a spot of color on the far end
and crossed the pit

to see it.

A lily stood there,
tall and vibrant and strong,
brightest orange
with brown spots,
its head bent over
like a turban.

Who had planted this
out here alone
in the wild,
and why?
I didn't pick it.
I'd grown past that even then,
but admired it silently,
then never mentioned it
to anyone.

Long after,
I found it in a field guide...
the Turk's Cap lily,
a true wild flower.
No person planted it.
It grew where it belonged
incredibly beautiful and alone,
where only the wild
things saw it,
and a child
who never forgot.

Nancy's Walls

The walls of Nancy's home are white...
cool, no-nonsense, unassuming.
But her quilts, her pillows, her life
add an aura of warmth...
as does the love she shares there.

The cat, driven by whatever insanity
infects the best of cats,
stood on his rear legs
and, reaching up as high as he could go,
pulled his claws down, down, down
with a satisfying feel and sound,
leaving beautiful lines in the once-pristine walls.
Then, having slaked his momentary madness,
went off to sit on the sofa and doze in the sun.

Cat-scratch white was not pretty.
But while Nancy pondered what to do
(after telling him that wasn't nice)
the cat got up, rubbed adoringly against her,
then went happily down the hall,
and found a place for a double set of gashes.

Could white on white work? the woman worried.
It might not match,
might stand out, look even worse.
And while she thought of what she could do
he slipped onto her lap to fall asleep.

One night when the moon was full,
he climbed on the sofa
and drew his claws down the wall behind it.
"Bad cat," the woman said on the following morning,
but her heart wasn't in it,
and when he went to her she hugged him.
While she stared at the gashes she saw
long, thin lines, like stems...stems...stems.

From a closet she pulled out some paints and stiff
    brushes,
painted soft green stems wherever he'd struck,
thin leaves that fluttered in an unseen breeze.
And on top, nodding and bent, but strong,
pink flowers blossomed.
She moved out the sofa, drew moss green pots,
and out of them raised more fine pink flowers
to peek over the couch where the cat liked to sleep.

Sometimes, like people, cats run through phases,
get some wildness out of their systems.
He is through with all that...his crime spree is over.

Pink flowers, simple things, peek around corners,
dance in the halls.
No sign left of ruin...just gentle, sweet flowers.

Snowflakes Falling on Ginkgo Leaves

Shifting winds
    rustle the oak leaves
        that won't let go their branches
but set the heaps of ginkgo leaves
    whirling
        where they've fallen.
Dancing...
    must be their very reason for being.
In spring
    when the sun was gentle
        and the rain was soft
they danced tremulously
    while robins made the music.
Flushing into the deeper emerald of summer
    the leaves lustfully caught
        every passing breeze.

But the delicate yellow leaves of October
    waved so strongly
        in the autumn gales
they whirled from the trees
making piles of restless sunshine
    on the grass
        where still they danced
in spurts of ebbing passion.
        Slowly fading
ghosts of unmet dreams
    fandangoed ever slower.

But sun goes white
    when the breezes chill
and large snowflakes fall
    quieting the leaves
        slowly...
putting a gentle end
    to the dance.

The Apple Tree
Beside Bradstreet Lane, Act II

She stands there still,
    though really she leans
at the edge of a meadow beside Bradstreet Lane,
near an old stone wall
    that is also more ragged
      than in its youth.
Her trunk, no longer smooth, is rougher
    and not as strong.
In places the bark is peeling.
And in the scar made by a broken branch,
a woodpecker drills a hole
    to make a home.
Valiantly she braves each season's storms,
    the lightning, winds,
      thick snow and sheaves of ice.
She faces them all unafraid
    even though they break her,
for tender memories of younger days
    keep her spirit alive.
She sees the field-edge pines
    grow taller, darker, and draw near.
The deer still pause in respectful obeisance.
And every spring she wears again
    the lush green foliage,
standing proud and beautiful once more,
    her youth restored.

But the flowers no longer come,
and the leaves aren't hers,
but the leaves of growing vines
    of bittersweet and poison ivy.
Come autumn, there are no apples
but like a gypsy she wears
    the bittersweet's gold and orange berries
    and the ivy's tiny gray pearls.
She weakens more,
and when she falls, the berry veils
will decorate the grave
    of a proud old lady.

The Mink

I met a mink one day
near Pintail Pond
where the water spills under Stone Bridge
and spreads out to flood the life-rich marsh.
He was on the bank looking up.
Our eyes met,
    two pairs of wild brown eyes...
Two sentient beings...alone
    but not lonely.

And time stopped.

The white winter sun paused in the sky,
and the breeze held its breath.
Life waited.

We watched each other
    with innocent curiosity.
I let my eyes slide from his face
    as his eyes flicked sideways.
Neither of us threatening nor threatened,
we kept each other in view
as we went about our business....
    looking for birds,
    looking for food.

I spoke to him at last...softly,
whispered words of respect and admiration,

words of love...for a brother.
At my words, he looked up
    to lock onto my eyes with his
    without threat,
    without fear,
then turned
    and sauntered further up the bank,
blended
    into the dried reeds and cat tails...
a smooth, dark, velvet movement
    that vanished
    even as I watched.

The Language of Snow

Pttt...pttt...pttt...
The small snow crystals
hit the beech tree's copper leaves
which won't let go until the springtime
brings back light and warmth and life.
Ping...ping...ping...
Half ice, half snow, they hit
the weary skier's goggles hard.
Almost home, the young man thinks,
but pauses by the frozen meadow
touched by the beauty.
Hisss...sss....sss...
The snow sifts down, straight down,
through the silent hemlock branches.
A fine sugar coating dusts the quiet grove
where the small herd of deer hunker down
to doze peacefully, secure and sated,
as the snow drifts steadily through the night.
Its kiss gentles them to sleep.

Slashing sideways, song of demons,
driven by a savage wind.
Smashing, bashing, unforgiving,
breaking, burying, killing,
mercy it holds out to none.
Raccoon peers out at the vicious world,
then snuggles deeper in his tree hole
while the devil winds howl the snow.

Tsk...tsk...tsk...
Lilting, laughing, tiny snowflakes
dance down from a whitened sky.
Softly landing, whirling, innocent,
each no bigger than a sigh.
But together, hour by hour,
they close the roads and bury fields.
And the fox no longer plays,
but hurries to his den to sleep.

Hush, hush, can you hear them?
Like a whisper the huge flakes come.
Unsure if they should land or flutter,
waltzing in the slightest breeze.
Touch the small boy's sleeve and stay there.
Make his eyes fill with wonder
at the beauty he cannot keep.
Woodchuck deep inside his burrow
barely breathing, dreams of spring.
Hush, hush, the dancing feathers
whisper, *It will come again.*

Chimney Swifts

44

Chimney Swifts

The chimney swifts came back last week.
From the headwaters of the Amazon they came.
I heard a twitter in the air,
looked up and saw two flying there,
cutting the air in jagged flight,
with mouse-like tweets they voiced the news...
At last...Spring!

They came that day
and then were gone.
They couldn't stop; so much to do,
a nest to build in a hollow tree,
or a chimney where they'd rather be.
But in the sky a promise hung
    They would be back...
    They had sung.

On that first day, just two flew in.
But late one afternoon,
more gentle voices stitched the air...
sometimes less and sometimes more.
Sometimes low they skimmed the yard,
but other times they flew quite high,
as if they yearned to touch the sky.
They dove and soared with mouths agape,
and scooped the insects from the air.
They rid us of all pests up there.

We used to watch them, he and I,
the gray birds reaching for the sky,
but that was very long ago.
I watch alone now.
   Still I watch,
and every spring they keep the faith.

Yet come late summer there is a day,
when I look up and have to say,
they've gone until another year.
They follow not the rules of men.
Come spring, they will return again.
And then their flight against the sky
will cheer me 'til the day I die.

Ebb Tide

Dead low
    quiet water
    endless hard sand to walk upon
a stillness seems to hold the sea back.
    Time has stopped.
Then minutely
the water begins to creep
at first imperceptibly
    it inches up the beach
and sandpipers run at its very edge
    chased higher and higher
    further and further up.

I remember the peak high tide
    on Plum Island one October day.
We were alone on the very tip of the land
alone all day.
No one else came down.
We didn't understand why,
    with such perfect weather,
but reveled in our isolation.
We didn't know the island
    had been closed since ten a.m.
We didn't know the circling helicopters
    were checking all the beaches
to warn people off...but missed us.

The surf grew wilder.

47

The rising wind blew back the spume.
The waves raced in
    like Chinese warrior horses...
    the white spray their wild manes
    tossing as they galloped into battle
    with the shore.

Our lips were salty from the spray.
Our skin flushed from the sun.
We didn't know that day for us
    was the start of forever.
We left before sunset
    the last people to get off the island
before it was cut in half
by the marauding warriors
    of an offshore storm's high tide.

And the tide began to turn.

It's running down, running out.
I feel it in every atom of my body
    and I am angry.
Growing older, slowing down
like the waves retreating further down the beach,
only the gentle slipping, ever lower.
The ocean and I move
always closer
to dead low.

The Water, Like Glass

Standing lonely
on the river bank,
I feel all my worries
slipping into the current
of the topaz-colored water.

The river Slade is quiet.
No canoes approach.
No paddles bang on metal sides
or splash the water.
If anything glides on the river
it is the ones who belong here,
moving silently,
the ones who live and breathe wilderness.

A laughing gurgle startles me,
and I move furtively along the shore
to quietly watch two otters
running up
and sliding down the muddy ramp.

I find a fallen log
and sit,
letting the calmness sweeten the air.
    I breathe
the air that nourishes me.
    I breathe.

Evening approaches
    softly.
A veery calls
    nearby...or from another dimension
    and I remember
the one who walked here with me once.

The water, like glass,
    is deceptive.
for as I look across the inlet
to the close-by channel islands,
it is not a mirror image that I see.
The current breaks reflections,
    destroying perfection.

I walk here alone now
    beside the river I love,
for the other does not walk beside me
And yet
    his image is almost there
        in the gentle current.

50

The Christmas Tree

Along the curbside it lies...waiting.
Shorn of its light
and tasteful/gaudy decorations,
empty of cheerful memories
and love.

He got it to stand securely
in the corner near the window
and strung the white lights.
Then, done with his yearly role,
he walked away, to watch the game,
feeling nothing.

Unrolling strands of tinsel, she began,
coolly, calmly, like an automaton,
stopping only once when she heard
the laughter of children
who were not there.

She moved on to the major decorations...
balls of red and gold and silver,
then personal memorabilia and homemade...
Beware!
The balls spaced high and low...
That was safe.
A Santa, glass candy canes, little snowmen,
a fairy, a little plastic rocket ship...
That one hurt.

A needlepoint frame with a boy's picture...
Don't look.
The girl's picture with a gap-toothed smile...
Why did the funny ones no longer made you laugh?

Icicles, last, dripped carefully one by one.
The girl, now far away with her own family,
always put them on with her, one by one.
But the boy who had helped so carefully at first,
preferred to toss handfuls.
"That's how real ice comes, in globs and sheets."
So the children lived their lives,
the girl, so carefully.
But the boy squandered his days
with doubtful friends, and hopeless dreams,
and drugs,
and giving up.

In two days people would be coming
to celebrate, as they always did,
to eat and drink and admire the tree.
"To absent friends," he would toast,
parents, friends,
their son.

She cast one last admiring look
at the tree
that shimmered through her tears.
Then all alone she stripped the tinsel,
tore all the icicles off in clutching handfuls.
The ornaments came next, all willy-nilly.

Jammed into boxes, a few were broken.
The star, she'd never gotten to it.
No matter, there were stars enough
moving in the cold realm of space.

He came back in, his camera ready,
and stared silently at the naked, ravaged tree.
His tears blended with hers...he never cried.
They held on to each other,
and heard the haunting laughter of a child.

Tatts

When I was young,
ladies didn't get tattoos
but then...
Pluto was a planet,
children played freely in their own back yards,
you could take a ride on a Sunday afternoon,
and man hadn't walked on the moon.

My husband had tattoos.
As an underage boy, lying about his age,
he went into the Navy
to save his family, his home, and his country.
Tatts, that's what the young salts got
(so young, barely children, trying to be men).
A bluebird on his ankle
I remember best. It suited him.

My time came later,
(after my nearest and dearest were all gone).
The dark days of numb terror
passed in a slate-blue haze
of appointments, procedures, and tests.
One long night in the spruce outside my window
an owl called,
and I shook with fear
    and unexpected anger.
Four small dots, the doctor said,
needed for thirty-six days

to guide the death rays of radiation
to the exact spot to kill anything left
and save my life.

Four small blue dots,
still there after fifteen years.
Like his bluebird, they're mine for life.

Blue tattoos...there is a time for everything,
and one way or another
we all come through life...marked.

Solitary Skater

Bunker Meadow has long been flooded
so that ducks can find a haven in the springtime
and is frozen now
to a safe depth.
But I only skirt the shore on my skates
not really afraid, but not yet sure enough
to venture further from the familiar
sanctuary of the land.

I plod through the feathery snow
and dream
trying to recapture another time
    long past,
    well past
a time when I
yet believed in miracles.
A time when I loved unafraid.

At the canoe landing,
I find a pile of old logs
spilled carelessly on the riverbank,
and sitting there, I drift safely
away again to that other time and place
only to hear...suddenly
the kiss...kiss of blades on ice,
and turn to see
one man skating.

He moves in idle circles,
here and there,
casual and vague.
If he sees me
he gives no sign
but only looks into another dimension,
where all creatures
see a kinder place to live.

Kiss...kiss.
His blades cut clean lines
as he moves over the frozen waters,
sketching the ice,
melting through the air,
knifing the solitude I seek there.

Kiss...kiss.
A wild goose calls
and the air is pregnant with snow.
Suddenly the solitary skater makes one last pass
silently
lifting his hand in a salute.

WITCH HAZEL

These November woods are pale with death,
offering only emptiness, brown and gray.
Thin ice that rims the river
is fragile now
but promises the solid shield
of winter.
All the fire of October has faded
to nothingness.

I, too, am empty, beyond feeling,
beyond hurt.
But the witch hazel is in bloom!
I almost miss
the tiny green-gold flowers,
gnarled blossoms thrusting upward
to reach the grayed-out sun.

I look around.
Death *isn't* here.
The trees, though bare, have strong, sheathed buds.
A squirrel, rushing by,
packs one last nut away,
ensuring life
until another springtime.
There is an all-pervading whisper of life.
The witch hazel won't be quiet,
and unafraid, flings forth its flowers,
wizened and green-gold.

There is a promise in these November woods.
The witch hazel pledges.
Out of the twisted, yellow flowers
comes hope.

The Swarm

THE SWARM

"It will come," the old man said,
    "if it comes,
    in August."
The child, who had seen only nine Augusts,
    fastened on the month
that in June seemed a million hours away.
While I held onto the word "if,"
    having known too many "ifs,"
    half of which had failed me.

Summer drowsed past,
    hot humidity yielding to dry, windy weather.
The child paddled her canoe
    under the old man's guidance,
and together they explored the river's
    hidden coves
    and tiny islands.
While I coddled flowers and vegetables
    nourishing life
    in the fecund garden.

The August sun spilled lime-green light
    that whispered, "Autumn coming"
    to the land
But when the day came at last,
    we had nearly forgotten
until the old man's call echoed up the stairs,
    "Come quickly...it's here!"

The child and I spilled out onto the lawn
where he was already waiting,
and the three of us just stood,
        awed and laughing, in the sun.
The ants, small golden notes,
were streaming out of their holes
and taking flight,
        a rapturous flight in the summer sun,
        and the gentle, warm air,
        a first and last flight
            to mate, and then to die.
But the squadrons came too,
        dragonflies...everywhere,
        golden, slate blue, cherry red,
        the huge green darners
        like miniature helicopters.
They darted, soared high,
skimmed low,
scooping the rapturous ants
into their rapacious jaws.

The child held out her arms and danced.
My eyes widened in wonder
as more and more dragonflies came in.
The old man smiled
as much at our joy
as at the squadrons of the summer.

As the sun began to sink,
        the frenzy lessoned.
The child caught a dragonfly with reverence,

and let him go.
A cherry red one landed on my arm
        in peace, and then flew off.

I remember golden notes in the air.
I remember three people
standing in a shower of life.
I knew...in that one, late afternoon
I held innocence in my heart and my hands.

To My Chinese Mother

My name is Emily, Emily Ruth Wagner.
I live with my parents, my adoptive parents,
in a white house beside the sea.
I've lived a happy life here,
but sometimes, when a silent fog
creeps up from the ocean,
I think of you so very far away.

My parents were told you carried me for two days
to officials who took the unwanted.
For two days you walked,
our skins touching.
Did you hurt, so fresh from childbirth,
knowing it would soon end,
that you would go home weaker, sadder,
and with nothing?

We will never meet in person.
China is so big.
So many people.
So many rules.
But I think by writing these words,
love and gratitude will carry them to your heart.

That someday in the fields,
or cooking supper,
or going to sleep,
you will feel a little starburst inside you

and know I am alive and happy,
and love you.

I will think of you the rest of my life.
Whenever I see a new mother cradle her baby,
or an older woman bent with age,
I will think of you.

When I have my own child and she is old enough,
I will tell her about you, her other grandmother,
who is lost to us...in time and space,
but not in heart.

Think of me often, if you can without pain.
Open yourself and let my love flow into you.

I know you loved me.
Twice...you gave me life.

The Wisdom of the Trees

For more than seventy years
I've seen New England's autumn trees,
relishing in the festive colors
that varied subtly each year,
reflecting weather changes
    and my sorrows, joys, and loneliness.
But not until this very year
did I at last understand their message.
So slowly does wisdom grow,
    if it comes at all.

That late October day, the trees
were glowing, making a feast for the eyes.
The leaves that had already fallen
made a thick, crunchy cushion
as I kicked my way through them.
Years fell away.
I was a child again.
The autumn sunlight was burnished by their richness,
which made the light alive and nearly dancing.
And though the bronze was tinged by cold,
the air was warmed by the luminosity
of the autumn trees.

I walked the quiet paths, bathed in their light,
at peace as the amber glow
washed over my eyes,
    stilled my mind,

    erased my worries.
Then, turning a corner,
in all this multiplicity of Midas hues, I saw
one tree.
Standing amid the ranks of all that beauty,
yet it drew itself apart.
And while I see it still
in a corner of my mind,
words fail to describe the shades of it.
Its color was a living thing,
a pulsing, vibrant blush.
It hurt my heart to look at it,
but I could not look away.
That one tree,
amid all the other's rich colors,
pierced deep inside my being,
and in that moment, I understood
the message of the autumn trees.

Before the driving winds and rains,
before the gentle, heavy snows,
the trees strive to tell us
if only we can understand their language.
Using their brilliant, throbbing tones,
they urge us to hold tight.
For even as our days surrender
to the dark and chill of winter,
and the death winds from the North
savage our world,
none of this will last forever.
The sweet days will come again.

So as the snow begins to fall,
and ice glitters from the eaves,
I hold in my heart the golden light of autumn.
And the memory of that achingly beautiful tree
will shimmer in my very core
  all the winter's long.

Viewpoint

the small herd of deer
allows me to approach unconcerned
I follow them with confidence
but silently they melt into the trees
    alone
      I am lost

up the steep esker
I climb eager for the view
stretching to the marsh and river
a skunk walks up from the opposite side
    rapidly
      I yield the way

the ground remains still frozen
and the cold March wind lingers into April
a mourning cloak butterfly
rises from the path to challenge me
    respectfully
      I turn aside

the fox in the snow-crusted field is playing
he throws a small brown animal up
then pounces on it again
the sun makes his coat glow
    quietly
      I sit watching

the vultures are riding a thermal
six of them circle and rise
over the hemlock forest
something is dying or dead they hope
    it is not my time
      I turn off the trail

sitting quietly on a log I almost
see a dark shadow pass nearby
I watch the tall grass blowing lightly
a face appears to watch me...the fisher
    admiring
      I speak to him

the night is cold and lonely
but overhead the three a.m. sky explodes
as meteor after meteor splashes across and dies
trails of light challenge the stars and are gone
    with wonder and gratitude
      I feel peace

BLUE SPRUCE

I am the elder lady
    child of foreigners
    sister of a simple brother
holding life tenuously beside my blue spruce.

My blue spruce guards me.
Tall, over the house, he reaches
every year a little higher
his branches, thick and heavy...strong.
My tree, the smoked blue-green shade
of forgetfulness.
My tree...tips his branches in springtime
with golden stars.
My tree I can reach from the upper windows.
My tree, whose three huge breaks,
have missed the house and hurt no one.

When my tree sighs, I sit beneath it,
hugging its shade on hot days,
sitting under its branches when I am sick,
watering its ground with tears when I grieve.
When my tree whispers,
    he tells me, do not be afraid.
When the killing wind makes his branches
toss and bend,
    he tells me, hold on old lady,
    but don't let go.
When he rustles

crows and blue jays settle in their nests
on his branches ... unafraid.
Because of him, I have grown
    from a shy girl to a strong old lady.
Because if him, I have been safe.

He is dying now;
bare branches shatter.
He is much older than I am.
Perhaps we'll share another year or two,
and then...and then...
I will cherish his final days,
our final days,
knowing, where love has grown,
the earth is sacred.

www.ingramcontent.com/pod-product-compliance
Lightning Source LLC
Chambersburg PA
CBHW051737040426
42447CB00008B/1175